# BALLOTS FOR BELVA

## The True Story of a Woman's Race for the Presidency

by Sudipta Bardhan-Quallen
illustrated by Courtney A. Martin

Abrams Books for Young Readers, New York

When Belva Lockwood was ten years old, she read that, with a little bit of faith, anyone could move a mountain.

She took the words literally.

Of course, Belva didn't try to move a whole mountain—after all, she was just a child. A hill seemed much more appropriate. She scouted around until she found the perfect one. She picked out a small hill outside her house and concentrated all of her willpower on moving it. She had faith in herself, and she was determined to move that hill, even if it was just the tiniest little bit.

The hill stayed put.

But Belva never stopped trying to move mountains.

Belva was born on a farm in Niagara County, New York, in 1830. She was the second of five children, and she described herself as "a simple country-girl" and "the daughter of a poor farmer." But humble beginnings didn't stop Belva from aiming high.

Years after the mountain-moving incident, after getting married, having a daughter, being widowed, graduating from college, working as a teacher, starting a suffrage group, and marrying again, Belva decided she wanted to be a lawyer. She was thirty-nine years old, smart, spirited, and willing to work hard. But no law school would admit her. One said:

> Mrs. Belva A. Lockwood:
> Madam—The Faculty of Columbian College have considered your request to be admitted to the Law Department of this institution, and, after due consultation, have considered that such admission would not be expedient, as it would be likely to distract the attention of the young men.

Two other law schools never even responded to her application. A mountain was blocking the way to her dream.

Belva set about to move the mountain—and this time she wasn't going to fail.

Belva heard about the newly formed National University Law School, where the school directors claimed that they wanted to open their doors to women alongside men. They invited Belva to attend the classes, along with fourteen other women.

But the school didn't make things easy for the women—they weren't allowed to go to the same classes as the men or to take their exams in the same rooms. Many of the men at the school didn't want any women studying with them, and they weren't afraid to show it. They grumbled to school officials that they wouldn't go to school with women. Twelve of the women dropped out of law school—it was just too hard to manage the pressures of school and the hostility from their classmates.

Belva was one of only two women to finish the coursework.

And after all that hard work, and though the women did everything that the men did, the law school wouldn't give the women their diplomas.

But Belva wasn't about to give up.

On September 3, 1873, she wrote a letter to Ulysses S. Grant, who was both president of the United States and president of the National University Law School:

*To His Excellency U.S. Grant, President U.S.A.:*
*Sir—You are, or you are not, President of the National University Law School.*
*If you are its President, I desire to say to you that I have passed through the*
*curriculum of study in this school, and am entitled to, and demand, my diploma.*
*If you are not its President, then I ask that you take your name from its papers,*
*and not hold out to the world to be what you are not.*
*Very respectfully,*
*Belva A. Lockwood*

A few days later, Belva got her diploma, signed by the president himself. She was now a lawyer.

She'd moved that mountain right out of her way. And she'd learned an important lesson: that she could accomplish anything she wanted with, in her words, "will-power and mental effort, combined with indefatigable labor." She knew that she would never stop believing, never stop thinking, and never give up.

Again and again, Belva
showed the world what she
could do, and when she did
something, others followed in her
footsteps. She was already the first woman
to graduate from National University Law School.
Over the years, Belva also became the first woman to
practice law in federal courts and the first to argue a case
before the Supreme Court of the United States. Within a year of
earning this right, Belva helped a black attorney, Samuel R. Lowery, gain
the same privilege. She believed as strongly in Lowery's equality before the law
as she had believed in her own.

Belva was a respected and influential lobbyist, public speaker, and activist
for women's rights. She was also the first to ride around Washington, D.C., on a
tricycle—an early type of bicycle with three wheels—very efficiently, too, since she
could speed along at ten miles an hour. Within two or three years of Belva's tricycle
debut, so many women were following her lead that the *New York Times* wrote,
"Now a woman on a tricycle attracts no more attention than a woman on a horse."

In 1884, at the age of fifty-four, Belva was first once again. She became the first woman to officially run for president.

At the time, women couldn't even vote. Belva had been working for many years to get laws passed to change that. She went to two Republican conventions, in 1880 and 1884, trying to convince the Republican Party to make women's suffrage a part of its official platform. Both times, Belva was ignored.

Belva was so frustrated that she wrote to the *Woman's Herald of Industry*, "Why not nominate women for important places? . . . It is quite time we had our own party, our own platform, and our own nominees. We shall never have equal rights until we take them, nor respect until we command it."

Belva realized that though women couldn't participate in elections by voting, there was nothing in the law preventing them from running for office. "I cannot vote," she said, "but I can be voted for."

So that's what Belva decided to do.

In August 1884, Belva received a letter from the Equal Rights Party of the United States that said:

*Madam:*
*We have the honor to inform you that you were nominated, at the Women's National Equal-Rights Convention, for President of the United States.*

Belva was shocked and surprised, and initially kept the letter a secret. But on September 3, she wrote back to accept the nomination. Her campaign began.

Belva selected another woman, Marietta Stow, to be her running mate. Democrat Grover Cleveland and Republican James Blaine were Belva's main opponents. The campaign would be difficult. It was very expensive to run for president, to travel across the country to campaign, and to make the campaign a full-time job—especially without the backing of a well-funded political party. In 1872 a woman named Victoria Woodhull had announced that she would run for president, but her campaign was suspended before Election Day because she didn't have the money to continue.

In those days there were no state-provided ballots that listed all the candidates' names. Instead, every political party had to print and distribute its own ballots, meaning that candidates or parties that didn't have enough money to print ballots couldn't get any votes. Belva had worked on presidential campaigns in the past, so she knew what needed to be done. She worked hard to raise money for her campaign by giving speeches all over the country, and she organized her supporters to get ballots ready.

Belva thought it would be a lively campaign— even though she knew there was a massive mountain between her and the White House.

By now, you know that mountains wouldn't stop Belva Lockwood.

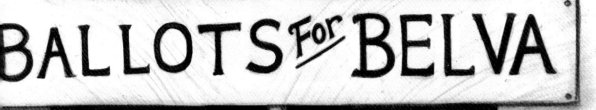

The Washington Post

LAUGHABLE LOCKWOOD

Lockwood v.s. Duniway:

Belva didn't stop when newspapers called her campaign "the most laughable masquerade this city ever witnessed." She didn't stop when male critics organized "Belva Lockwood Parades," where they dressed in women's clothing and pretended to be her.

She didn't even stop when she ran into trouble in places she didn't expect. She had spent most of her life working for women's rights—in fact, she was running for president in part to convince people that women should be able to vote—but many women opposed her run for president. Some women thought she was crazy to try to force herself into what most people considered a man's world. Others, who believed in women's rights as deeply as Belva did, thought she was making a spectacle of herself and was making a joke out of the fight for women's rights. The National Woman Suffrage Association, the most important women's rights group, told Belva it would not support her run for president. In fact, one suffrage leader, Abigail Duniway, said, "The damage done by her . . . cannot be estimated."

In August 1884, Belva received a letter from the Equal Rights Party of the United States that said:

*Madam:*
*We have the honor to inform you that you were nominated, at the Women's National Equal-Rights Convention, for President of the United States.*

Belva was shocked and surprised, and initially kept the letter a secret. But on September 3, she wrote back to accept the nomination. Her campaign began.

In 1884, at the age of fifty-four, Belva was first once again. She became the first woman to officially run for president.

At the time, women couldn't even vote. Belva had been working for many years to get laws passed to change that. She went to two Republican conventions, in 1880 and 1884, trying to convince the Republican Party to make women's suffrage a part of its official platform. Both times, Belva was ignored.

Belva was so frustrated that she wrote to the *Woman's Herald of Industry*, "Why not nominate women for important places? . . . It is quite time we had our own party, our own platform, and our own nominees. We shall never have equal rights until we take them, nor respect until we command it."

Belva realized that though women couldn't participate in elections by voting, there was nothing in the law preventing them from running for office. "I cannot vote," she said, "but I can be voted for."

So that's what Belva decided to do.

But Belva still had her faith. She knew she was doing something important. If nothing else, people were listening when she spoke—and Belva spoke about all the things that were important to her. In speech after speech across the nation, she told her audiences that all Americans deserved equal rights, regardless of their race or gender.

People listened. Quite a few people, in fact. The editors of the *Washington Evening Star* eventually wrote that "it is evident that Mrs. Lockwood, if elected, will have a policy [which] will commend itself to all people of common sense."

On Election Day, Belva didn't have much to do. After all, she couldn't go to the polls and cast a vote—not even for herself. She waited in her Washington, D.C., home, opening it to any reporters who wished to interview her.

She and the nation learned that Grover Cleveland won the election.

But Belva won votes.

Belva didn't win just a few votes—she won 4,711 popular votes, cast in nine out of the thirty-eight states that existed at the time. And those were only the ones that were counted at all. There were more votes for Belva, especially in Pennsylvania, but those were thrown away because the vote counters couldn't believe anyone would actually vote for a woman.

Just when it looked like Belva had accomplished what she had set out to do, after the election she found out about the good number of her votes that were thrown away. She also learned that in some cases her votes had been given away to other candidates. In fact, many of Belva's votes from the state of New York—a total of 1,336—were counted for Grover Cleveland. Cleveland won the state by only 1,149 votes—and Belva wondered what would have happened if her votes hadn't been miscounted.

She petitioned Congress about voting practices in January 1885, saying that because the government did not control the ballots printed for an election or properly oversee polling places, people could easily stuff ballot boxes with fake votes or destroy or not count votes that had been legally cast.

It didn't do much good. Congress didn't change the vote tallies.

But Belva knew that whether Congress accepted her candidacy or not, she had moved that mountain as far as it would go at the time. Belva had become the first woman who ran for president who actually got people—men, since they were the only ones voting—to cast their ballots for her. She was the first woman to prove that Americans were willing to consider a female president.

Belva believed that someday a woman would become president of the United States. She said, "If [a woman] demonstrates that she is fitted to be president she will someday occupy the White House. It will be entirely on her own merits, however. No movement can place her there simply because she is a woman. It will only come if she proves herself mentally fit for the position."

When it was time, the mountain would move all the way. And Belva had given it a huge push.

All it took was "will-power and mental effort, combined with indefatigable labor." And Belva's determination to show the world what a woman could do.

# Author's Note

Belva Lockwood had strong beliefs and wasn't afraid of failure. That's probably why she had the courage to try so many things. Belva broke barriers all throughout her life. For example, when she was seventy-five years old, Belva represented a group of Cherokees in a case that was appealed to the Supreme Court, *Cherokee Nation v. United States*. Federal troops forced these Native Americans off their lands in North Carolina, Georgia, and Tennessee, but the tribe members were never compensated out of the fund created by the U.S. government from the proceeds of the sale of Cherokee land. Belva won the Cherokees a settlement of $5 million—a staggering sum, even today.

In her 1884 presidential bid, a good number of people voted for Belva. The formal tally varies from source to source, ranging between 4,149 and 4,711 popular votes. But voting officials admitted that many of Belva's votes were thrown out, so the number is likely higher. It is very impressive that Belva got any official votes—she was the first woman in history to do so.

Presidential elections aren't decided on popular votes, though. Our system uses electoral votes. Every state has a certain number of electoral votes, and generally, the candidate who wins the popular vote in a state is awarded all of that state's electoral votes. But there is no rule that says states have to award electoral votes to the popular vote winner.

In 1884 the electors in Indiana informed Belva that they decided not to award Indiana's electoral votes to the candidate who had won the popular vote in that state, Grover Cleveland. Instead, they told Belva they had cast their electoral votes for her, even though no woman had ever won electoral votes in a presidential election.

The *Indianapolis Daily Sentinel* reported that the Indiana electors' decision to change their vote was meant to be a joke played on Belva. But the historical record shows that Belva did not take it as a joke. After a presidential election, the electoral votes of each state must be certified by Congress. When Congress declined to award Indiana's electoral votes to Belva, tallying them for Cleveland, Belva fought them based on what she had been told by the Indiana electors. She petitioned Congress that Indiana "had an undisputed right" to vote for her.

The members of Congress didn't change anything based on Belva's petition. But they didn't laugh it off, either. They referred Belva's petition to the Committee on Woman Suffrage, making it an official part of the congressional record.

Regardless of the election's outcome, one of Belva's finest hours was when she was nominated for president. She ran once in 1884, and then a second time in 1888. But was Belva really the first woman to run for president? It depends on how you look at it.

In 1872 a woman named Victoria Woodhull was nominated for president, also by the Equal Rights Party. Historians disagree, however, on whether Woodhull received any votes in that election. No official votes were recorded for Woodhull. In addition, there is some dispute about whether Woodhull's name appeared on ballots all around the country.

Belva Lockwood's votes were undisputed. Records exist supporting Belva's popular votes and her nearly awarded electoral votes. Because of this, Belva remains the first woman to officially receive votes in a presidential election.

Interestingly, Belva achieved another first with her run for president—she was the first candidate to have a female vice presidential running mate. Geraldine Ferraro, who was Democrat Walter Mondale's running mate in 1984, is widely considered the first woman to run for the vice presidency. The truth is, Ferraro was the first woman to represent a major party, but Marietta Stow, Belva's running mate, was the first woman to run for vice president.

Throughout her life, Belva encouraged other women to work for their rights. She believed in the equality of men and women, and that the United States would eventually grant all of its citizens equal protection under the law.

She was right.

# Glossary

*Ballot*: A piece of paper that a voter uses to mark his or her preference for a candidate in an election.

*Convention*: A meeting of all members of a political party to discuss the party's goals, decide on the party's positions on different issues, and sometimes pick a candidate for a particular election.

*Elector*: A person selected to be a part of the Electoral College.

*Electoral College*: The group that directly votes for the president. Once the popular votes have been counted in each state, the electors meet to cast their votes.

*Electoral vote*: A vote cast by an elector. In the United States, each state is assigned a certain number of electors, and the popular vote in each state usually determines how the electors vote for the presidency.

*Petition*: A formal request, often signed by the people making it, that is addressed to a person or group in a position of power and asks for rights, favors, or benefits.

*Platform*: A public summary of a political party's goals, objectives, and positions.

*Popular vote*: The votes cast by all eligible citizens.

*Suffrage*: The right to vote.

# Women's Suffrage in the United States

**1780s**
&#10003; **1787:** During the U.S. Constitutional Convention, it is determined that the states could decide on voting qualifications. All states except New Jersey take away women's right to vote.

**1800s**
&#10003; **1807:** The right to vote is taken away from women in New Jersey, the last state to revoke it.

**1830s**
&#10003; **October 24, 1830:** Belva Ann Bennett is born in Royalton, New York.

**1840s**
&#10003; **1848:** The first U.S. women's rights convention takes place in Seneca Falls, New York. The "Declaration of Sentiments and Resolutions," outlining the goals for the women's movement, is signed.

**1850s**
&#10003; **1854:** As a college student at Genesee Wesleyan Seminary and Genesee College (later Syracuse University), Belva first hears suffragist Susan B. Anthony speak about women's rights.

**1860s**
&#10003; **1866:** Elizabeth Cady Stanton and Susan B. Anthony join together to form the American Equal Rights Association (AERA), dedicated to gaining universal suffrage for women and African Americans.

&#10003; **1866:** Belva moves to Washington, D.C., and becomes active in political groups like the AERA.

&#10003; **1867:** Belva becomes one of the founders of the Universal Franchise Association, Washington, D.C.'s first suffrage group.

&#10003; **1868:** The Fourteenth Amendment is ratified, extending the protections of the Constitution to all "citizens"—specifically defined as "male" — against unjust state laws.

&#10003; **March 11, 1868:** Belva marries Ezekiel Lockwood.

&#10003; **1869:** The Wyoming Territory grants women the right to vote within its borders, the first time American women had suffrage since 1807.

&#10003; **May 1869:** The National Woman Suffrage Association (NWSA) is formed. Elizabeth Cady Stanton is its president.

&#10003; **November 1869:** The American Woman Suffrage Association (AWSA) is formed. Henry Ward Beecher is its president.

**1870s**
&#10003; **1870:** The Utah Territory grants women the right to vote. They lose this right in 1887.

&#10003; **January 1870:** Belva attends the NWSA convention in Washington, D.C., where she meets other influential suffragists such as Elizabeth Cady Stanton.

&#10003; **1872:** Susan B. Anthony attempts to vote for Ulysses S. Grant in the presidential election. She is arrested and brought to trial in Rochester, New York, in June 1873. In addition, in Battle Creek, Michigan, Sojourner Truth appears at a polling booth and demands a ballot, but she is sent away.

&#10003; **1872:** Victoria Woodhull is nominated for president by the Equal Rights Party, but she suspends her campaign before Election Day. She does not receive any official votes.

**1870s cont.**

✔ **May 1873:** Belva graduates from National University Law School.

✔ **January 10, 1878:** The "Anthony Amendment," which is named for Susan B. Anthony and which aims to give women the right to vote, is introduced into the United States Congress. It fails to be passed.

✔ **February 15, 1879:** H.R. 1077, a bill drafted by Belva allowing women to argue cases in front of the Supreme Court, is signed into law by President Rutherford B. Hayes.

**1880s**

✔ **February 2, 1880:** Belva sponsors Samuel R. Lowery, an African American man, to practice before the U.S. Supreme Court.

✔ **November 30, 1880:** Belva argues the case of *Kaiser v. Stickney*, becoming the first woman lawyer to appear before the Supreme Court.

✔ **November 1884:** After running as the presidential candidate of the Equal Rights Party, on Election Day, Belva receives over four thousand votes.

✔ **May 1888:** Belva is nominated for president again by the Equal Rights Party. Overall, she receives fewer votes than she had in 1884.

**1890s**

✔ **1896:** Idaho grants women the right to vote.

**1900s**

✔ **1906:** Belva represents the Eastern Cherokee Indian Nation in a lawsuit against the U.S. government for a treaty violation that led to the 1838 "Trail of Tears" relocation of the tribe. The case is heard before the Supreme Court, where Belva wins an award of $5 million for her clients.

**1910s**

✔ **1910:** The state of Washington grants women the right to vote.

✔ **1911:** California grants women the right to vote.

✔ **1912:** Theodore Roosevelt's Progressive (Republican) Party adopts the cause of women's suffrage to its official platform, becoming the first national political party to do so.

✔ **1912:** Oregon, Arizona, and Kansas grant women the right to vote.

✔ **1913:** The Alaska Territory grants women the right to vote.

✔ **1916:** Jeannette Rankin of Montana becomes the first woman to win election to the U.S. House of Representatives.

✔ **1917:** North Dakota, Indiana, Nebraska, Michigan, and Arkansas grant women the right to vote in limited capacities. New York, South Dakota, and Oklahoma grant women the right to vote in all elections.

✔ **May 19, 1917:** Belva dies.

**1920s**

✔ **August 26, 1920:** The Nineteenth Amendment, with the same wording as the 1878 Anthony Amendment, is ratified, granting women the right to vote throughout the United States.

# Selected Bibliography

Brown, Drollene P. *Belva Lockwood Wins Her Case*. Morton Grove, IL: Albert Whitman & Company, 1987.

Cook, Frances A. "Belva Ann Lockwood: For Peace, Justice, and President." Women's Legal History Biography Project, Robert Crown Library, Stanford Law School. 1997. http://womenslegalhistory.stanford.edu/papers/LockwoodB-Cook97.pdf.

Fox, Mary Virginia. *Lady for the Defense: A Biography of Belva Lockwood*. New York: Harcourt Brace Jovanovich, 1975.

Lockwood, Belva A. "How I Ran for the Presidency." *National Magazine*, March 1903.

——. "My Efforts to Become a Lawyer." *Lippincott's Monthly Magazine*, February 1888.

Norgren, Jill. "Before It Was Merely Difficult: Belva Lockwood's Life in Law and Politics." *Journal of Supreme Court History* vol. 23, no. 1 (1999): 15–42.

——. "Belva Lockwood: Blazing the Trail for Women in Law." *Prologue Magazine* vol. 37, no. 1 (Spring 2005) http://www.archives.gov/publications/prologue/2005/spring/

——. *Belva Lockwood: The Woman Who Would Be President*. New York: New York University Press, 2007.

Stern, Madeleine B. and Belva Lockwood. "Two Unpublished Letters from Belva Lockwood." *Signs* vol. 1, no. 1 (Autumn 1975): 269–275.

To my daughters, who can move mountains. —S.B.Q.
With love to my family and friends, who remind me anything is possible. —C.A.M.

Library of Congress Cataloging-in-Publication Data:
Bardhan-Quallen, Sudipta.
  Ballots for Belva / by Sudipta Bardhan-Quallen ; illustrated by Courtney A. Martin.
    p. cm.
  ISBN 978-0-8109-7110-3
  1. Lockwood, Belva Ann, 1830–1917—Juvenile literature. 2. Women presidential candidates—United States—Biography—Juvenile literature. 3. Presidential candidates—United States—Biography—Juvenile literature. 4. Feminists—United States—Biography—Juvenile literature. 5. Women lawyers—United States—Biography—Juvenile literature. I. Martin, Courtney A., ill. II. Title.
  E664.L68B37 2008
  305.42092—dc22
  [B]

                              2007049842

**HNA** ▪▪▪ ▪  115 West 18th Street
harry n. abrams, inc.  New York, NY 10011
a subsidiary of La Martinière Groupe  www.hnabooks.com